COMPASS
True Stories for Kids

CAPE BRETON COAL MINERS

FIGHT ON!

1900–1925

Joanne Schwartz

NIMBUS
PUBLISHING LTD.
—— NIMBUS.CA ——

Nimbus Publishing Limited
3660 Strawberry Hill, Halifax, NS, B3K 5A9
(902) 455-4286 nimbus.ca

Printed and bound in Canada
Library and Archives Canada Cataloguing in Publication

Quote on page 12 used with permission from the publisher. From Frank, David. "Contested Terrain: Workers Control in the Cape Breton Coal Mines in the 1920s" in *On the Job: Confronting Labour Process in Canada*. Eds. Craig Heron & Robert Storey. Montreal: MQUP, 1986.

Quotes from John Mellor's *The Company Store* and Rennie MacKenzie's *Blast!* are used with kind permission from Ronald Caplan, publisher of Breton Books.

Editor: Penelope Jackson
Editor for the press: Emily MacKinnon
Cover and interior designer: Andrew Herygers

Library and Archives Canada Cataloguing in Publication

Title: Fight on! : Cape Breton coal miners, 1900-1925 / Joanne Schwartz.
Names: Schwartz, Joanne (Joanne F.), 1960- author.
Series: Compass (Nimbus Publishing)
Description: Series statement: Compass : true stories for kids | Includes bibliographical references and index.
Identifiers: Canadiana (print) 20200172174 | Canadiana (ebook) 20200172301 | ISBN 9781771088565 (softcover) | ISBN 9781771088572 (HTML)
Subjects: LCSH: Strikes and lockouts—Coal mining—Nova Scotia—Cape Breton Island—History—20th century—Juvenile literature. | LCSH: Coal miners—Nova Scotia—Cape Breton Island—History—20th century—Juvenile literature. | LCSH: Coal mines and mining—Nova Scotia—Cape Breton Island—History—20th century—Juvenile literature. | LCSH: Coal miners—Labor unions—Nova Scotia—Cape Breton Island—History—20th century—Juvenile literature.
Classification: LCC HD5329.M615 S39 2020 | DDC j331.892/82233409716909042—dc23

Nimbus Publishing acknowledges the financial support for its publishing activities from the Government of Canada, the Canada Council for the Arts, and from the Province of Nova Scotia. We are pleased to work in partnership with the Province of Nova Scotia to develop and promote our creative industries for the benefit of all Nova Scotians.

*For Cape Breton miners and their families
and the incredible communities they created*

"I believe in telling children the truth about the history of the world, that it does not consist in the history of Kings and Lords and Cabinets, but consists in the history of the mass of the workers, a thing that is not taught in the schools.
I believe in telling children how to measure value, a thing that is not taught in any school."

—J. B. McLachlan, 1925

Table of Contents

Look up definitions to terms in **bold**
in the glossary, starting on page 64.

A pickaxe and bucket of coal.

Introduction

Look at the map. Cape Breton sits at the northeastern corner of Nova Scotia, separated from the mainland by the Strait of Canso. Rugged coastlines carve out its shores as the land rises north to the Highlands, jutting into the

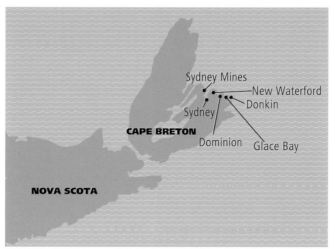

Cape Breton Island, the eastern part of the province of Nova Scotia.

Atlantic Ocean. This small island has a big history. This small island is full of stories.

The Mi'kmaq were in Cape Breton first, living sustainably on the land for thousands of years. By the 1500s Portuguese and Basque fishermen reached the island's shores, attracted by the abundance of codfish. By the 1600s the French and English began creating permanent settlements, occupying land and claiming it was theirs. The battle for **colonial** power ended in the defeat of the French at Louisbourg in 1758, which led to British rule.

Cow Bay, 1873, now Port Morien, opened the first commercial coal mine in North America in 1720 and supplied coal to the Fortress of Louisbourg.

In the late 1770s, Highlanders, forced off their land in Scotland, began arriving in Nova Scotia looking for a new start. The first permanent Scottish settlement in Cape Breton was in Judique in 1775. Then, between 1815 and 1850, thousands more Scottish settlers made the difficult crossing and landed on the island. Despite the tremendous hardships they faced, the Scottish settlers put down roots and became fiercely attached to their newly adopted home. Their Celtic culture flourished in small rural communities scattered across Cape Breton. Fishing and small-crop farming provided a modest living. It was a way of life not so different from the Scottish Highlands, until coal mining changed the course of history. A story as rugged as the coastlines began to unfold.

Cape Breton has large deposits of coal, a resource that in the early 1900s was in huge demand. Formed over millions of years, thick layers of coal stretch for miles under the sea. The coal deposits are so abundant that inky black coal seams, called **outcrops**, can be seen running along the cliffs.

One of the earliest uses of coal was by the French at the Fortress of Louisbourg. The exposed **seams** of coal made it

Coal, a fossil fuel in abundance in Cape Breton, has had a dramatic impact on the history of the region.

readily available, and the first mine was set up in Cow Bay, what is now Port Morien, in 1720. Over the next century, small-scale mining continued. The development of mining on a larger scale really began with the General Mining Association in 1826. This

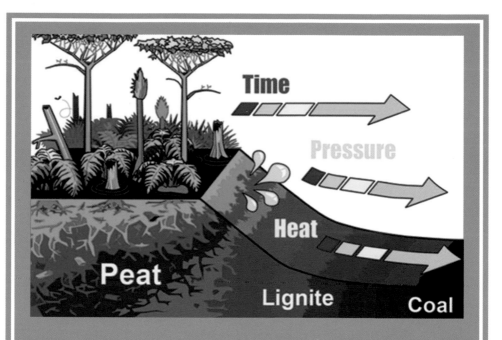

Coal is formed from plants that grew over 300 million years ago in swampy forests. Ferns, reeds, and mosses grew, died, and then fell into the swamp. As more and more plants died, they formed layers of rotting vegetation. As the earth's conditions changed, rocks, sand, and rivers compressed the layers of dead plants, squeezing out the water and burying the vegetation even deeper. Coal slowly forms in four stages. The first stage of coal is called peat. With more pressure, the peat turns into lignite coal, the second stage. The third stage, bituminous coal, is the result of even more pressure, with very few signs of vegetation left. The last stage is anthracite coal, a hard, shiny coal formed from pressure and heat. Bituminous coal is what was mined in Cape Breton. Coal is some-times referred to as "buried sunshine" because of the energy from the sun trapped in the plants for millions of years.

Fight On!

was a sign of what lay ahead. The huge deposits of fossil fuel in Cape Breton were about to ignite the dramatic history of **industrialization** on the island. Coal mining had always been a dangerous industry. Coal mining in the underwater mines of Cape Breton in the early decades of the twentieth century reached a high-pitch of dangerous, unfair, and **repressive** working conditions. Labour struggles became an important part of the island's history.

As the twentieth century dawned, Cape Breton was a booming and industrializing coal-mining region. **Industrial capitalism** had appeared quickly as the nineteenth century came

Coal miners at Dominion No. 1 Colliery, early 1900s.

Dominion Colliery No. 2, Glace Bay, 1912. The colliery included these buildings on the surface and the mine underground.

to a close. Towns sprouted overnight, like mushrooms after the rain. A way of life that had existed without capitalism was gone forever.

How did this situation come to be? In 1893 the provincial government sold most of Cape Breton's natural resources off to a **corporation**. Henry Melville Whitney, an American industrialist, formed the Dominion Coal Company and was granted a ninety-nine-year lease for all untapped coal deposits in Cape Breton. Despite Whitney's big plans for the region, he sold the company by 1909. It was taken over by a group of entrepreneurs in Montreal and Toronto. Far from the **coalfields**, these greedy

INTR. B. F. BOILER HOUSE.
THE DOMINION IRON & STEEL CO., L.
DEC. 23, 1900. NO. 416 SYDNEY C.B.

Coal and steel

During Whitney's time in Cape Breton, he also built the steel plant in the Whitney Pier area of Sydney. Coal was a key ingredient in making steel, as was the iron ore from nearby Newfoundland. Whitney saw the opportunity for more profits by creating a second industry that would use coal from his Dominion Coal Company. In 1899 Whitney formed the Dominion Iron and Steel Company and began building the steel plant, which was finished in 1901. The region was suddenly bursting with jobs, but from the beginning, the wages paid to the men who would make steel and dig coal were the lowest priority for the company owners. These businesses were about making big profits, and those would always come at the cost of a **living wage** for the workers.

entrepreneurs ran the company without any care for the welfare of the miners who took the coal from the ground. Workers, families, and their communities were like cogs in a wheel, part of the machinery of corporate growth.

What did that mean? It meant that the Mi'kmaq, their traditional way of life destroyed, would be further mistreated, eventually forced onto reserves by the 1920s. They would not be a part of the coal-mining industry. It meant that the rural culture of the Scottish immigrants who came in the 1700s and 1800s, hoping for a better life, would be changed forever as they were forced to move into the towns to find work. It meant that industrial corporate

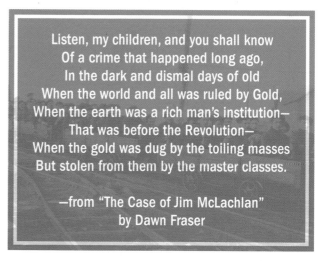

Listen, my children, and you shall know
Of a crime that happened long ago,
In the dark and dismal days of old
When the world and all was ruled by Gold,
When the earth was a rich man's institution—
That was before the Revolution—
When the gold was dug by the toiling masses
But stolen from them by the master classes.

—from "The Case of Jim McLachlan"
by Dawn Fraser

capitalism was beginning to thrive and the lives of working people would feed its endless hunger for resources, growth, and profit. It meant that the industrial barons of the early twentieth century would become unimaginably rich because of the unimaginably hard work of the miners and their families. It meant that conditions in the mining towns would reach such levels of poverty that families would be living on the streets and children would go hungry. It meant that the company's disregard for the safety of working conditions in the mines would lead to the loss of many lives. It meant struggle, starvation, and death for the workers. The miners of Cape Breton would spend many long, hard years fighting for the right to a living wage and safe working conditions.

Dawn Fraser

Dawn Fraser
ECHOES FROM LABOR'S WARS
THE EXPANDED EDITION

Dawn Fraser's working-class poetry

Dawn Fraser (1888–1968) was a well-known figure in Glace Bay in the 1920s, especially for his labour poetry. He used his poetry to tell the story of working-class life and criticize the injustices of industrial capitalism in Cape Breton. His poems described the poverty and the suffering of miners and their families and the greed of the corrupt bosses; they paid tribute to the sacrifices of labour leaders like J. B. McLachlan; and they documented the events of the labour wars in fiery language. Fraser would often read his poems aloud at **union** meetings, on street corners, and at strike rallies. They would be posted around town and printed in the labour paper, the *Maritime Labor Herald*. He was known as "a fierce voice for justice."

CHAPTER 1
Life in the Mining Towns

What the mines were like

What is most striking about the Cape Breton coal deposits is that they stretch deep under the ocean. To reach the coal deposits, the mines extended from the cliffs for miles under the sea. The **colliery** buildings, standing tall on the shorelines, were like icebergs, exposing only the very tip of the colliery.

Bankhead at Dominion No. 6 Colliery in Donkin, 1920.

Fight On!

Glace Bay, 1905. This photo shows the terrible working conditions deep underground in the mine for both humans and animals.

A main **shaft** was sunk at a steep angle from the ground to access the coal seams. It led to tunnels that sloped away two or three miles under the ocean. This type of mine was called a submarine mine. The underground workings of the mine were a maze of rooms and tunnels that spread out over an area as big as twelve to fourteen square miles. It was so vast that there could be a blast in one area of the mine without miners (also called colliers) in another area even being aware that it had happened. It was a dark and dangerous place to work.

Miners would be transported from the **bankhead** down the dark tunnels on a **rake**—empty coal cars that would be used for bringing coal back up to the surface. Using a buddy system, they would pair off and make their way to their "room." The walk from the rake to their room could be a mile long. Here, the men would begin a backbreaking day of work hacking at a seam of coal with a pickaxe. They would not get paid for the time it took to get to their room or for how many hours they worked; they would just

"The miners' workplace was unusual in many ways. The miners worked in a labyrinth of dark slopes, tunnels, and caverns located hundreds of feet below the surface of the land and ocean. In their travel to work and in their daily tasks, the coal miners confronted harsh physical conditions: rough footing, steep grades, a low roof, dripping water, narrow passageways, pools of stagnant water and mud, cold rushing air currents, clouds of bitter smoke and choking coal dust, falling stone and coal overhead, fatal pockets of methane gas embedded in the seams, and finally an almost universal darkness."

—David **Frank**

get paid for how much coal they brought to the surface. Their day of work was measured by their strength and endurance.

It was often said that coal miners never saw the sunshine. They woke to a 5:00 A.M. whistle, walked to the **pithead**, worked twelve hours, and went home exhausted at 6:00 P.M. In the winter months they would indeed not have seen any sun. Family life revolved around the miners' schedule. Miners' wives were

Fight On!

Pit Ponies

Pit ponies were small, sturdy miniature horses that did important work in the Cape Breton mines. Just like the miners, pit ponies had a difficult working life and spent most of it underground. The ponies were used for hauling boxes of coal. Once a miner had worked the coal surface, he would fill a box and lead the horse up the long tunnel to where the boxes would be hitched to a winch and steel rope and pulled up to the bank-head. Back and forth they would go for long shifts. The miners took very good care of the ponies, keeping them well-fed and their underground stables as clean and comfortable as possible. But the pit ponies' lives were very hard.

It wasn't until the 1940s, when the miners were finally allowed a two-week vacation, that the pit ponies got one too. They would be brought up to graze for two weeks above ground. Sometimes the horses had to wear blinders until their eyes got used to the bright sunshine. The last pit pony in Cape Breton came out of the mines in 1960.

up even before 5:00 to make breakfast and pack a lunch. In the worst of times, lunch could be just bread and molasses. Packed in a metal lunch bucket called a piece can, that and a Thermos of tea were all the miners had for their long, hard shift. Miners' children grew up knowing their fathers as tired men whom they only saw for a few hours at the end of the day.

Children working

In the early twentieth century, it was normal for children to work. Boys were a large part of the mining workforce. They were important wage earners for their families, especially if a father or an older brother had died or been injured in a mining accident. Some boys went **down the pit** as young as anywhere from

Boy miners at Caledonia mine in 1903. In the early 1900s, boys as young as nine went down the pit.

Fight On!

nine to thirteen. For those young boys, school was over and their working life had begun.

Boys did a number of different jobs at the collieries, although most of them were trappers. That meant they would sit in the dark for hours and hours beside a trapdoor and wait until they heard a miner coming along the tunnel. Then they would open the door to let the miner come through with his box of coal being hauled by a pit pony, then close it quickly so dangerous gases couldn't gather. Although opening and closing the door was simple, controlling the airflow was a matter of life and death in the mines. For the whole day, boys would sit alone in complete darkness, with only rats for company. Boys also worked at the bankhead, where the coal was poured from the coalboxes onto screens. As the screens rumbled past, the boys scrambled to separate the coal from the stone and shale. Coal dust swirled around them like fog, and the possibility of serious hand injuries was very high. The boys would do this exhausting, dangerous work for ten hours at a time for a very low wage.

Girls' and women's lives

Women were the backbone of the community in the coal towns. Their unpaid labour took place in the home and included running the household and bringing up the children. Women's work started early in the morning and continued throughout the day. Coal dust was everywhere in the towns and it was a constant job to keep the houses clean, scrubbing floors and washing walls.

15

Basic chores like laundry required hard physical work and took two days of each week. Women needed to boil water on the stove, transfer it into a washtub, and then scrub with soap on a washboard. When the clothes were hung outside to dry, they often got dirty again just from the soot and coal dust in the air. Once the clothes were dry, the women would then iron, darn, and patch to make them last as long as possible.

Trying to feed a family on starvation wages was another challenge. Women had to find ways of stretching their tiny budget. They needed to be thrifty and resourceful, so they grew vegetables, kept chickens and cows and pigs, made their own clothes, and were expert recyclers, finding a second and third use for every single item. Like boys who followed their fathers into the pit, girls were expected to help their mothers with domestic labour.

Women didn't just stay at home, though; they also actively supported the struggle for labour rights. Being the accountants in the family and partners in the struggle, they discussed with their husbands union issues and contracts. Women marched in strikes, they joined demonstrations, and they made their voices heard, demanding justice for the coal towns. During times of strike, in winter or summer, they set up soup kitchens and helped to organize fundraising drives. In the 1920s, women's labour clubs were set up in many of the mining communities by women committed to working for labour reforms.

You Are Invited

Bean Supper

UNION HALL, NEW ABERDEEN
Under Auspices of

Ladies' Labor Club

Mon. March 24

AT 7 P. m.

Admission 25c.

Women Hold Well Attended Social at New Aberdeen

NEW ABERDEEN, May 12.—The Women's Club of New Aberdeen held a most successful Box Social tonight. -The purpose for which these social evenings are put on is that the working women may get to know each other and enjoy an evening every once in a while away from the eternal grind that is the usual thing in the life of th ordinary working class wife and mother.

While they keep an eye on the social end they do not forget the practical end for which the women have organized, that is the political advancement of the working class as a whole. To this end, after all expenses of the social, it is understood the women placed in their funds a nice round sum against the day when the Armstrong government can find courage enough to appeal to the voters of this province.

Will done for the women! They helped out this Labor Paper, helped out the May Day Celebration—in fact made tha. day the succes, that it was. Now after having helped others in such a practival way, we are glad to see them do so well for thei. own Club.

Advertisement for a community bean supper put on by the Women's Labor Club, and article congratulating them on a great success, both of which appeared in the *Maritime Labor Herald* in 1924.

One of the hardest things women and girls in a mining community had to face every day was the possibility that their husbands, brothers, or sons might die in a mining accident. If that happened, even through their grief, they had to find a way to manage on their own. The women participated in the miners' struggles, suffered the miners' poverty, and fought to build the community.

Company houses, company stores

To house the workforce for industrial-scale mining, company towns appeared—and with them, a way of life that kept the miners forever in debt to the corporation. Sydney Mines, Dominion, Glace Bay, and New Waterford changed from small settlements to overcrowded towns almost overnight. Company houses were thrown up, spreading out in rows from the collieries like octopus tentacles. The conditions in the growing towns were terrible. And living in a company house meant that when miners went on strike, the company could evict them, throwing families out on the street.

The typical company house was built as cheaply and quickly as possible. Each house had a thin wooden divider in the middle, splitting the house in two. This created a "double" house,

Coal company houses were poorly built and quickly became run-down.

Fight On!

with a family living on each side. There was no insulation, no electricity, no running water, and no indoor toilets. Water had to be hauled from a nearby well for household needs. Because miners had no money for repairs, it didn't take very long for the poorly built houses to start falling apart. The thin walls provided very little protection against the long, bitterly cold Cape Breton winters.

The company store, famously called the "pluck me," was owned and operated by the company. It was the main store in town to purchase groceries, dry goods, bedding, and just about anything else needed for a household, and it was also where the miners had to buy their work clothes and equipment. The store

19

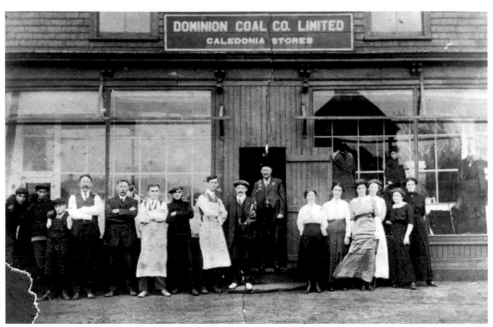

Dominion Coal Co.'s Caledonia company store and employees. The company store, nicknamed the "pluck me," was the main store in town. Items bought on credit were taken off a miner's paycheck at the end of the month.

The company store had everything—groceries, dry goods, and clothing, as well as many tempting items that a miner's family couldn't afford.

Fight On!

worked on credit: miners' wives could buy things as needed and the money was taken off their husband's next paycheque. The miner and labour leader J. B. McLachlan called the women "the greatest financiers of the world," yet no matter how they tried to save money, they couldn't make the budget work. By the end of the month when a miner collected his wages, they amounted to almost nothing. That was where the name "pluck me" came from. A miner's hard-earned money went right back into the corporation. And when the miners went on strike, credit was cut off at the company store. With no money to go elsewhere and no credit, the miners could be starved back to work.

Company towns were built around the company, which meant there were few other places to work. Despite the terrible working conditions, miners had few options if

The bob-tail sheet was a weekly account of a miner's wages and deductions. Against the wages, the company deducted what was spent at the company store and the rent, heat, and light for the company house. Other deductions included expenses for the doctor, hospital, and church.

they lost their job or became injured. As credit was built up at the company store, they had to stay to pay off their debt. Some new immigrant miners without work simply left town. But most miners had long-established roots and didn't want to leave their communities. Fighting for workers' rights was also a commitment to fighting for the rights of the community.

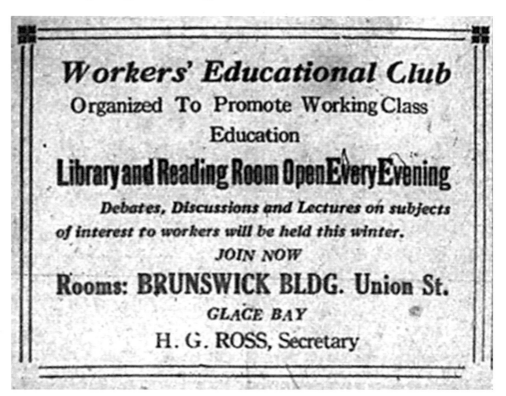

Advertisement in the *Maritime Labor Herald*, 1924.

Fight On!

CHAPTER 2
J. B. McLachlan

One person became very important in the lives of coal miners and their families. James Bryson McLachlan arrived on the shores of Cape Breton on a steamer in the winter of 1902. Born into a working-class family in Scotland, he, like so many others, had to leave school at the age of ten and go to work in the mines.

Even then McLachlan was a serious boy. He was known to carry a book around the colliery with him, reading whenever he could, determined to continue his own education. He grew up working in the mines, and it wasn't long before he became involved in the struggles for workers' rights. By the time McLachlan was thirty-three and married with four children, he was **blacklisted** from the Scottish coalfields. He had to find work to support his family, and so he was forced to leave Scotland. Like many migrant

James Bryson McLachlan, a Scottish immigrant, became one of the most important labour leaders in Cape Breton.

workers from Europe, McLachlan was following the trail to the Cape Breton coal mines, looking for a new start. He would be shocked to find the collieries of his new home were even further behind in labour reform than the ones he had left behind. J. B. was to become a central figure in the Cape Breton mining struggles. He rallied the miners and led the fight for working conditions and wages that valued people and community over profits and wealth.

Building a strong union

McLachlan's struggles began with his work to bring a more powerful union than the Provincial Workmen's Association (PWA) to Cape Breton. The PWA, established in 1879, cooperated with Dominion Coal to keep workers from striking. McLachlan looked to the United Mine Workers of America (UMWA) as a union that would support stronger action by the miners. The timing was important, because the 1905 contract, which had already set the miners' wages far below the cost of living, was ending. Dominion Coal wanted it to be renewed without any wage changes, even though the cost of living had risen 20 percent since 1905. McLachlan knew this was an important time to strike, and he wanted to be able to put up a united front. He held a **referendum** and the miners voted strongly in favour of moving to the new union. Despite all efforts by the PWA to stop the UMWA from growing, local branches sprouted up throughout Cape Breton. The most famous was District 26 in Glace Bay, formed in March of 1909, with McLachlan voted in as secretary-treasurer.

Fight On!

The fight with Dominion Coal

Having fought for a new union, McLachlan was facing an even bigger battle with Dominion Coal itself. The financiers tried to stop the growing movement toward the UMWA. Every miner who joined one of the new UMWA lodges was fired. Company police and spies attended UMWA meetings. The situation was so bad McLachlan called for a Conciliation Board to be formed to stop the discrimination against union members. The government did create a board, but the board was deeply on the side of Dominion Coal. The unfair relationship between the government, the corporation, and the justice system would get in the way whenever McLachlan fought for the rights of the working class.

The offices of the Dominion Coal Company were in Glace Bay, the most important mining settlement in the region.

J. B. McLachlan

The company still wouldn't recognize the UMWA. Miners felt that they had the right to choose their own union, and when the company got in the way, the miners decided they had to strike. On July 6, 1909, they walked out.

The 1909–1910 strike

The coal company's response to the strike was to send in 625 special constables to protect the property of the Dominion Coal Company and intimidate the miners. The company built high fences around the collieries and hired labourers who were willing to work while others were striking. These labourers were called "**scabs**."

Then the company began evicting the fired UMWA miners from their company homes. The company police would barge into a house without knocking, order the family out, and throw their few personal belongings out onto the street after them.

The Dominion Coal Company was using intimidation, threats of jail sentences for striking miners, evictions, and use of scab labour to try to force the strikers back to work. McLachlan and the other executives of District 26 continued to try to meet with the coal operators. The company continued to ignore their requests.

Dominion Coal, determined to scare the workers, asked a judge to allow troops to be sent to Glace Bay. Within days, five hundred soldiers arrived armed with machine guns. The community reacted with anger and protest. McLachlan asked the

Dominion colliery, winter 1907. Train cars filled with coal and ready to be transported.

striking miners to remain peaceful. In a show of unity, the workers planned a march from Glace Bay to the neighbouring town of Dominion for July 31. About three thousand striking UMWA miners walked in protest, waving banners and singing striker songs. But as they reached Cadegan's Brook, they were forced to stop. There, waiting on the steps of the Immaculate Conception Church, were soldiers ready to shoot into the crowd. The strikers turned around and walked back to Glace Bay, unwilling to risk being hurt or killed. The use of the military in the mining communities was shocking, and it showed just how much the

J. B. McLachlan

Sent to Cape Breton during the 1909 strike, soldiers from the Canadian Army guard the property of the Dominion Coal Co.

corporation saw workers' rights as something to fight against no matter what.

The strike dragged on for months, and as 1910 began, it was a bitter, cold winter in Cape Breton. The situation for the miners and their families was increasingly dangerous. Families were living in tents, with barely enough food or clothing. Cholera, scarlet fever, diphtheria, and other diseases broke out, taking many lives, especially those of young children and old people. Starvation and disease affected everyone.

Fight On!

But all the suffering had no effect on the coal company. Ten long months passed, making it the longest strike in Cape Breton history. Finally, in April, it came to an end. Most of the UMWA workers were taken back to work, but the company didn't compromise in many other ways. It had been a long road for small gains. Throughout the years to come, the workers' resistance, struggle, and **solidarity** against corporate power would be their greatest achievements as they continued to fight for working conditions and wages that would meet the basic needs of a working-class family.

> So the capitalist class owned all the gold,
> And they also owned the goods that were sold,
> Controlling the workers in every way,
> And they grew greedier day by day;
> 'Til they thought of a little scheme was good—
> They raised the prices of all the food,
> So that the workers with pay they got
> Couldn't pay for the goods they bought;
> Couldn't pay for the bread or meat
> That they and their families needed to eat;
> Though they worked long hours and longer yet;
> There were things they needed and couldn't get;
> But the capitalist class had many things—
> Motor cars and diamond rings—
> Yet all these riches wherever found,
> Were dug by the workers from the ground,
> Were stolen from them by this thieving band—
> Such was the law in all the land.
>
> —from "The Case of Jim McLachlan"
> by Dawn Fraser

McLachlan's generosity

Identified as one of the key organizers of the strike, McLachlan was blacklisted from the mines, just as he had been in Scotland.

J. B. McLachlan

Miners heading underground on the "rake," empty coal cars, at Donkin, 1925.

His days underground were over. He could no longer work as a miner in Cape Breton. That meant he would have more time to fight for working people.

Unfortunately, the small amount of money paid to McLachlan for his work as secretary-treasurer of District 26 was not enough to support him, his wife, Kate, and their nine children. He had to find another way to make a living. With the generous help of UMWA members, McLachlan borrowed enough money to buy a small piece of land on the outskirts of Glace Bay. He and Kate set up a dairy farm there and grew vegetables. They now had a small source of income and a source of food for the family.

The farm produced enough milk and vegetables to sell, but they seldom got paid in cash. Because of the company-store policy,

Fight On!

miners and their families had almost no money, so McLachlan would trade them milk and vegetables for whatever they could offer. McLachlan was very kind. His daughter told of the time her father came home with an old pair of shoes on. When asked what happened, McLachlan told his story, which is recorded in the book *The Company Store*: "Well, Katie, I'll tell you. This

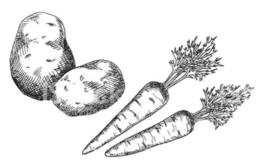

poor fellow, he's getting married, and he came up to me and asked me if I'd give him five dollars so they wouldn't have to walk to church. Well I stretched it a bit and gave him ten; and the shoes he had on were a disgrace." So, McLachlan had given the young man his own shoes and ten dollars! McLachlan's countless acts of generosity were legendary.

J. B. McLachlan

CHAPTER 3
Explosion in the Mines

When the First World War began in 1914, there was a much higher demand for coal production. Coal was the fuel for factories across the country, which were making weapons and equipment for the war effort. The Cape Breton coalfields were producing as much as they could. Profits boomed during the war, especially as the company inflated the price of coal to record high levels. Miners were working harder than ever and still struggling for a living wage.

During the war years, the fight for recognition of the new union, led by McLachlan, continued. Two miners' organizations, the PWA and the United Mineworkers of Nova Scotia (UMWNS) finally came together and formed the Amalgamated Mine Workers (AMW) of Nova Scotia in June 1917. It was a stronger and more united union. With profits high, the AMW's demands for wage increases were successful. Because there had been so few wage raises in the past, though, the increases were still not enough to cover the cost of living. And the workers were about to experience yet another injustice.

Fight On!

Draegermen, like those pictured here in 1909, were a volunteer team of miners specially trained in rescue and emergency procedures. The name comes from a kind of breathing apparatus, designed in Germany, which enabled someone to walk through the **afterdamp** of a mine explosion. The draeger team went down the pit when there was an explosion, fire, or accident of any kind to rescue the miners. They faced many dangers—toxic gases, fire, smoke, collapsed walls, debris, and incredible heat. The first draeger team in Cape Breton was formed in Glace Bay in 1907. Draegermen were highly regarded for their incredible bravery.

The whistle of woe

At 7:30 in the morning on July 25, 1917, a sharp, ear-piercing whistle blew through the streets and houses of New Waterford. Everyone knew what it was: the dreaded "whistle of woe," signalling a mine disaster. Every person in town was worried, because the sound of that whistle meant lives lost—whose and how many remained to be seen. There had been an explosion at No. 12 colliery. The whistle brought everyone running to the pithead to wait for news of their husbands, brothers, and sons.

It was hours of terribly anxious worry and then, for many, tragic news. It turned out to be the worst mining disaster in Cape Breton history. Sixty-two miners died in the explosion.

Death for profits

A rescue team worked to bring up all the miners who were underground during the explosion. McLachlan was one of the rescuers. Bringing bodies up from the depths to waiting relatives at the pithead was dangerous, exhausting, and heartbreaking. Three miners who had been on the surface and went underground to help with the rescue effort also died, bringing the day's death toll to sixty-five.

When it was all over, McLachlan went home smelling of the afterdamp from the mine. His daughter asked him what the terrible smell was, and McLachlan said, "That smell, Eva, is death for profits!" As was so often the case, McLachlan's words spoke to the dark truth of the Dominion Coal Company's attitude: miners' lives meant nothing, and profits meant everything.

The eight-hour workday

One of the many rights McLachlan was fighting for was an eight-hour workday, which already existed in Britain and the United States. Given the mining conditions and the demanding physical work involved, a twelve-hour workday was very hard on miners' bodies. It also gave them little time for family and community life. After years of the company ignoring calls for an eight-hour workday, McLachlan led a one-day work stoppage on July 8, 1918. Workers won their demand and the eight-hour workday was written into the 1919 contract.

Fight On!

No safety

The New Waterford explosion of 1917 was particularly tragic because of what had led to it. In an inquiry following the disaster, the jury found that the company had badly neglected safety precautions. Ignoring reports from miners, the company had allowed high levels of bad gas to collect. It was just a matter

Mining disasters in Cape Breton

Rennie MacKenzie, a former miner himself, knew firsthand what dangers a miner had to face each day he went down the pit. In his book *Blast!*, MacKenzie lists eighteen major disasters in the history of Cape Breton mining. MacKenzie defines a major disaster as an event where three or more lives were lost. Hundreds of accidents where one or two miners lost their lives are not included in this list.

1877: Lingan, boiler explosion	3 died
1878: Sydney Mines, explosion of gas	6 died
1892: Victoria Mines, boiler explosion	3 died
1899: Glace Bay, fire and explosion in Caledonia Mine	11 died
1903: Reserve Mines, gas explosion in No. 5 colliery, south level	5 died
1907: Little Bras d'Or, Scotia No. 4, runaway coalbox	3 died
1907: Glace Bay, boiler explosion No. 2 and No. 9 Surface Plant	4 died
1908: Port Hood Mine, explosion in No. 3	10 died
1911: Florence, gas explosion in No. 3	8 died
1917: New Waterford, explosion in No. 12	65 died
1924: Inverness, fall of stone in No. 1	4 died
1937: Sydney Mines, runaway trip in Princess Colliery	3 died
1938: Sydney Mines, runaway rake in Princess Colliery	21 died
1943: New Aberdeen, coal tank accident in No. 2 Colliery	4 died
1944: Glace Bay, speeding rake in Dominion No.1B Colliery	3 died
1946: Glace Bay, bump in Dominion No. 2 Colliery	4 died
1952: Glace Bay, gas explosion in No. 20 Colliery	7 died
1979: Glace Bay, explosion in No. 26 Colliery	12 died

of time before an accident would occur, one that could have been prevented if the company had followed the safety precautions. Mining was dangerous, but the company's disregard for safety greatly increased the chance of disaster and lost lives. As McLachlan would say, there was "blood on the coal."

Black Lung

Miners faced many dangers when they went to work. They could be pinned under a rockfall, exposed to toxic gases, injured or killed in an explosion, trapped in a fire, or caught on a runaway rake. Another type of injury, just as serious, was one a miner couldn't see: Black Lung, a disease so common to miners it is known as coal workers' 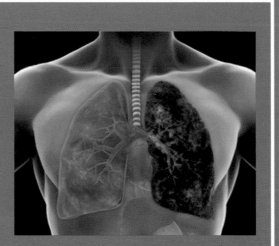 pneumoconiosis. The disease, caused from exposure to coal dust, slowly builds over years of working in the pit. The coal dust attaches itself to the walls of the lungs causing inflammation and scarring. The damaged lungs no longer work properly, leading to a persistent cough and difficulty breathing. A miner with black lung suffers a great deal and will eventually die from the disease. There is no cure. Many former miners in Cape Breton still suffer from the effects of Black Lung.

By 1919, after the explosion two years earlier, the AMW rejoined the United Mine Workers of America, the union that had replaced the PWA years before, hoping to put themselves in a better position to deal with the stormy waters that lay ahead.

Fight On!

CHAPTER 4
Roy the Wolf Takes Over

When the First World War ended in 1918, demand for coal dropped dramatically. The miners were only getting a few days of work a week. Returning soldiers couldn't find work. Once again, the families in the coalfields were in difficult times. With the cost of living still rising, there was a serious need to raise wages. After years of fighting, workers were still not receiving a living wage, and now times were harder than ever. As the 1920s began, conditions in the coal-mining towns were tough.

Plummer Avenue, New Waterford, the main street of the town, 1915.

Roy the Wolf

In 1920, when it seemed like the situation was as bad as possible, there was a change in management that would make the miners' lives even worse. Roy Mitchell Wolvin took over the

Dominion No. 6 Colliery, Donkin, 1920, men working on the surface.

British Empire Steel Corporation (BESCO).

Fight On!

newly named BESCO, the British Empire Steel Corporation, which merged the coal and steel companies into one huge corporation, promising great profits to its **investors**. This promise was built on "watered stock," which meant the value of the stock was inflated so that companies seemed like they were worth a lot. This dishonest move was typical of Wolvin, who had a bad reputation for his business practices. In his dealings with the Cape Breton miners, Wolvin would come to be known as "Roy the Wolf." His complete disregard for the miners and their families would turn out to be worse than they'd ever imagined. Once again, the miners would be battling the company's greed. After everything the miners and their families had gone through, their worst years were still ahead.

The first contract talks with Wolvin took place in a fancy Montreal hotel. Here, McLachlan would sit across the table from Roy the Wolf and demand a fair wage. As he walked toward the meeting room,

> Now, of all the bosses that e'er were cursed,
> Roy the Wolf was called the worst,
> He was the leading parasite
> That fed on the workers day and night;
> Greedy, growling wolf for more,
> He stole the bread from the workers' door,
> Grew fat on starving children's cries
> And filled the papers with foolish lies—
> That his company couldn't afford to pay—
> Yet he got three hundred dollars a day
> For doing nothing but looking wise,
> Starving kids and telling lies;
> Thus he promoted the capitalist game
> 'Til babies were taught to curse his name,
> And Roy the Wolf and his thieving band
> Spread distress throughout the land.
>
> —from "The Case of Jim McLachlan"
> by Dawn Fraser

McLachlan felt as out of place as a fish out of water. He wrote about what it felt like to walk on the glossy, elegant floors of the hotel:

> *The floor in this hotel seemed to jeer and laugh at me as I walked over it. If I walked on its carpet my feet sunk up to the shoe-tops. If I walked on the sides, where the carpet did not cover, I would slip and stumble and slide as if I walked on polished glass. This floor sure was class-conscious. It seemed to shout out at me: "Can't you see you're out of your element! Feet black and dirty from the coal mine should not walk here. I am for the gentle feet of idle men and fine women which are never soiled by labor." This floor, too, made me mad. Oh, if the miners from Glace Bay's wind-swept shacks could only have one walk over this floor, how it would make them fighting mad!*

McLachlan knew that the men in that room knew nothing of the working life.

A royal commission had been set up to look at the mining situation, and its recommendations for wage increases had an impact on the Montreal discussions. Wolvin was forced to make changes that would do a little bit to address the huge gap between wages and the postwar rise in cost of living. The one-year agreement was voted on and accepted by the union, which meant the miners could finally stop fighting for a short while.

Fight On!

Roy the Wolf

But Roy the Wolf was not happy to have made even these small changes, especially with profits declining. He was determined to raise company earnings by cutting wages, and he wanted to break the union as well. The following year, when the agreement expired, he wasted no time in announcing drastic wage reductions—33 percent starting in January 1922! There was outrage across the mining communities. This was nothing less than starvation wages. Nobody could survive on such a small amount of money.

All levels of government ignored McLachlan's appeals for help. No one was interested in taking care of the miners and their families if it risked the corporation losing profits. The union had to respond to this injustice. McLachlan led the miners in a slow-down strike, hoping this would avoid a full strike. Instead of producing as much coal as they could, the miners protested by slowing down their coal production so the company couldn't make as much money.

Spring and summer dragged on. Roy the Wolf refused to bargain. Just as in 1909, the miners had no choice but to strike. In August of 1922 the miners walked out, and this time it was a 100 percent strike. This meant that the maintenance workers also walked out, leaving the mines at risk of filling up with water and gases. The miners hoped this would force the company to work toward a settlement. Once again, military troops were sent to the coalfields to protect BESCO's property. This was an aggressive and unnecessary act by the government toward the Cape Breton miners. It wasn't the first time and it wouldn't be the last.

Fearing damage to the mines, Wolvin was forced to make a deal. The new terms proposed an 18 percent cut in wages instead of 33 percent. It was not great news, but it was a small improvement. The strike was over, and the men returned to work.

J. Simms, Trapper Boy Badly Hurt in No. 10 Mine

RESERVE.—John Simms, a 16-year-old trapper in No. 10 mine at Reserve, was seriously injured on Saturday morning when he got caught in a trip. Simms was carried along for a considerable distance and was bruised about the body and hear when he struck low roof. He was rushed to St. Joseph's Hospital, where he is being treated. It is believed that he will recover.

That it is the wear and tear of human life goes on in the coal mines of Nova Scotia, amongst youth and old age alike. Cheap coal is the constant cry of the boss; cheap (?) even if it is flecked with the blood of boys of the most tender years.

Maritime Labor Herald, 1924.

The *Maritime Labor Herald*

In these hard times, McLachlan wanted to give workers an independent voice. He started a newspaper for the working class called the *Maritime Labor Herald* (*MLH*), "a paper devoted

Fight On!

to labor," to engage and inform the workers. The first issue was published in October 1921. McLachlan filled the pages of the paper with the reality of miners' lives. He described what wage cuts really meant in the day-to-day-life of a mining family. He wrote angrily against injustice and encouraged workers to continue their fight:

There is in Glace Bay a married man with six children, four of them school age. This man works every day, and draws $2.85 a day in pay. He trades at the company store. His pay is so small and the price of articles so high, he cannot make ends meet. His four children have no shoes. The Company Store will give him only groceries and foodstuffs for his paycheck. The children therefore cannot go to school. The school authorities are threatening this worker with the penalty of the law for not sending his children to school. He cannot send them bare foot and scantily clothed in the winter months, and he cannot get them shoes and clothing. This worker is only one of many in the same plight. The Dominion Steel Corporation for which these workers work make millions of dollars a year in unearned revenues. Dan McDougall is said to draw $75,000 a year as his salary and Roy Wolvin is said to draw $100,000 a year as his salary. Millions of dollars and huge salaries to the parasites, ragged, hungry, and shoeless children of the wealth producers, who are denied an education because the father is paid so little wages, these are Cape Breton conditions.

If a miner was making $2.85 a day, working four days a week, he made around $600 a year. Out of that, rent, coal, light, and food (all paid to the company) were deducted from his pay. This left a family of six to eight people with almost nothing to live on. Meanwhile, Wolvin and his executives gave themselves huge salaries. Compared to the families in Cape Breton, they lived like kings.

The perils of publishing

The *Maritime Labor Herald (MLH)* was an angry voice for workers. In an editorial on the front page in 1924, the paper criticized the company, its owners, and the system:

> *The Maritime Labor Herald is openly the avowed enemy of capitalism and the capitalist class. We do our damndest in every issue to help drive the plundering crew from place and power and put them to work to earn an honest living.*

It was not by accident that the office of the *MLH* was set on fire four times between 1921 and 1925, twice burning the building down to the ground. McLachlan continued to publish with each setback but eventually, after a few lively years and having faced many obstacles, McLachlan put out the last issue in July 1926.

Fight On!

Maritime Labor Herald

WEEKLY

Vol. 2 No. 39 $2.00 PER YEAR   Glace Bay, Nova Scotia, Saturday, July 7, 1923.   FIVE CENTS COPY   No. 91

COAL MINERS STRIKE AGAINST ARMED FORCES

Mines In Cape Breton Tied Up In Protest Against The Use Of Armed Forces Against The Steel Workers Of Sydney

Maritime Labor Herald, 1923.

The steelworkers' strike

As 1923 began, the situation was becoming just as awful for the steelworkers. The Dominion Iron and Steel Company was also part of BESCO, and Wolvin was as mean to the steelworkers as he was to the miners. Because they didn't have someone like

The army on guard at the steel plant during the steelworkers' strike of 1923.

McLachlan fighting for them, the steelworkers didn't even have the right to be in a union. Anyone involved in union activities was fired and blacklisted.

The steelworkers reached their breaking point on June 28, 1923. They put down their tools and walked out. Wolvin immediately asked the province of Nova Scotia for a special police force to deal with the striking steelworkers. The troops arrived in Sydney on July 1. Only two days after the strike began, on a quiet Sunday evening, the police force charged on horseback into Whitney Pier, the area surrounding the steel plant. With clubs and sticks, they beat men, women, and children walking home from church and socializing with their neighbours.

It was a shocking event. The following day, in a letter to all miners' locals within District 26, McLachlan described what had happened and called for all locals to join in the fight against the company's violence and the Nova Scotia government's cooperation:

> *On Sunday night last these Provincial Police in the most brutal manner rode down the people at Whitney Pier who were on the street, most of them were coming from Church. Neither age, sex or physical disabilities were proof against these brutes. One old woman over seventy years of age was beaten into insensibility and may die. A boy nine years old was trampled under the horses' feet and his breastbone crushed in. One woman was beaten over the head with a police club and gave premature birth to a child. The child is dead and the woman's life is despaired of. Men and women were beaten up inside their own homes. Against the brutes the miners are on strike.*

Fight On!

McLachlan also sent the letter to D. H. McDougall, the vice-president of BESCO. McLachlan and the miners demanded that the troops be removed from their towns. To show complete support, the miners went on a sympathy strike in solidarity with their fellow steelworkers. On July 3, they walked out.

McLachlan goes to jail

The company and the government of Nova Scotia seized McLachlan's letter and used it as an opportunity to charge him with what they called "seditious libel." This meant they were accusing McLachlan of encouraging others to damage the property of the government of Nova Scotia. McLachlan and Dan Livingston, president of the union, who had delivered the letter, were picked up by the police and taken to the Halifax

Dorchester Penitentiary, New Brunswick, in 1900. This is where J. B. McLachlan was sent to serve his six-year sentence for seditious libel.

County Jail. For twelve days they were kept in a small, filthy, cold, bug-infested cell. With little food, no bed, open toilets, and crowded cells, it was easy for prisoners to catch diseases. McLachlan and Livingston already had lungs weakened by years underground, and now, unknowingly, they were

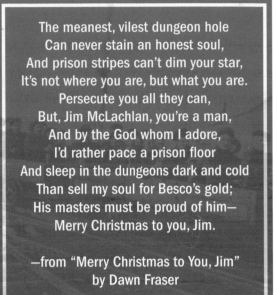

The meanest, vilest dungeon hole
Can never stain an honest soul,
And prison stripes can't dim your star,
It's not where you are, but what you are.
Persecute you all they can,
But, Jim McLachlan, you're a man,
And by the God whom I adore,
I'd rather pace a prison floor
And sleep in the dungeons dark and cold
Than sell my soul for Besco's gold;
His masters must be proud of him—
Merry Christmas to you, Jim.

—from "Merry Christmas to You, Jim"
by Dawn Fraser

exposed to pulmonary tuberculosis, which would eventually be the cause of both their deaths.

On July 20, McLachlan was released on bail. In an effort to raise awareness of the issues and to raise money for his defence fund, McLachlan went on a speaking tour across the country. Everywhere he went, crowds of workers came out to hear his fiery speeches. In October, McLachlan was back in Halifax sitting in a cell again, waiting for his trial. Justice Mellish was the judge and Colonel Harrington was the defence lawyer. Much of the case against McLachlan was an attempt to show him as a "Red," meaning a Communist—they accused him of being a dangerous revolutionary who wanted to overthrow the government of Nova Scotia. His house had been illegally searched and

Fight On!

his reading material was used against him as evidence of his Communism. Never mind that the company had starved the miners, lied about its "watered stock," brought in scab labour, and called out a special police force that had brutally attacked the community. McLachlan had allegedly said, "The property of the Dominion Coal Company can go to hell." According to the justice system of Nova Scotia, that statement was a worse crime than any of the company's actions, and for expressing that idea, McLachlan was found guilty of seditious libel. He was sentenced to six years in Dorchester Prison and taken immediately into custody.

The papers all had held a piece,
How men were beaten by the police;
Every father, mother, brother,
Had told the story to each other.
Yes, everywhere about the street,
Any man that you would meet,
Would tell the truth—could not be hid—
An awful thing those policemen did;
Story was told, re-told, attested,
But McLachlan only was arrested;
Yes, he and just one other man
Whom the workers called "Red Dan."
But soon O'Hearn let Dan go,
Which only served to better show
How all the tyrants' hate was sped
At noble Jim McLachlan's head.

—from "The Case of Jim McLachlan"
by Dawn Fraser

Released

There was a huge labour outcry across the country over McLachlan's sentence. Other workers created campaigns, petitions, protests, and appeals to free him. Four months into the sentence, he was granted "official remission," which meant he did not have to finish the rest of his prison term. McLachlan's release

Maritime Labor Herald, 1924.

was scheduled for March 4, but he stayed an extra day to finish making a pair of shoes for another prisoner. McLachlan made two stops on his journey home to Cape Breton. The first was in New Glasgow, where huge crowds of cheering miners came out to show their support; the second was in Sydney, where he was greeted again by an equally large crowd.

For his arrival home in Glace Bay there was a brass band, a parade, and streets lined with miners celebrating his return. At every stop, McLachlan spoke passionately against the injustices of the system and the need to stand up against corporate power. Prison had done nothing to stamp out his spirit.

CHAPTER 5
The 1925 Strike

As 1924 approached, the miners' contract was once again coming up for renewal. Wolvin announced he wouldn't allow any wage increases. With miners working only a few days a week, and wages far below the standard of living, this was unacceptable. How could families manage? There had been strikes in 1922 and 1923 and now, in January, in the depths of winter, miners went on strike once again. This time, instead of sending troops, the provincial government stepped in to force discussions. The result was a contract that made Wolvin give tiny wage increases but also included anti-union demands, such as not allowing workers to go on a 100 percent strike. It was not a good contract, and it was only meant to last a year. The strike ended, but everyone knew that the fight would come again soon enough.

In January of 1925, the miners were facing the contract renewal. Demand for coal continued to decline, and in order to pay investors, Roy the Wolf announced wage slashes yet again. The union refused to accept the proposal. As they debated what to do, the miners continued working. Then, on March 2, Roy the Wolf cut off credit at the company stores. Workers and their families relied on credit to be able to make ends meet with such low wages. He was cutting them off from their only source of food, clothing, shelter, and other necessities.

This was meant to threaten the miners and stop them from striking. But Roy the Wolf underestimated the miners' anger, and his decision had the opposite effect. Now the miners had nothing to lose. Facing starvation for themselves and their families, they called a strike, determined to stand up against Roy the Wolf. The strike began at 11:00 P.M. on March 6, 1925.

McLachlan and the miners chose a 100 percent strike, the same tactic used in 1922, to try to bring a quick end to the strike. The only place maintenance workers remained was at the power plant outside of town at Waterford Lake. The power plant supplied electricity to the mines and, just as importantly, electricity and water to the entire town of New Waterford.

Poverty in the coal towns was now widespread. Families did whatever they could to help each other. Relief stations were set up to distribute any

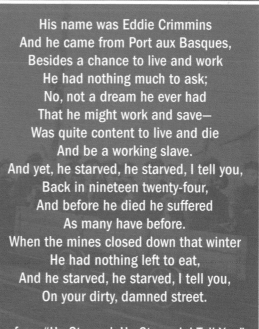

His name was Eddie Crimmins
And he came from Port aux Basques,
Besides a chance to live and work
He had nothing much to ask;
No, not a dream he ever had
That he might work and save—
Was quite content to live and die
And be a working slave.
And yet, he starved, he starved, I tell you,
Back in nineteen twenty-four,
And before he died he suffered
As many have before.
When the mines closed down that winter
He had nothing left to eat,
And he starved, he starved, I tell you,
On your dirty, damned street.

—from "He Starved, He Starved, I Tell You"
by Dawn Fraser

Fight On!

food people could share. Fish was free, so people ate a lot of it. Keeping the company houses warm without coal from the company store was another serious problem in March. People resorted to "bootlegging" coal, which meant digging for coal wherever a coal seam was exposed. It was as illegal as stealing a loaf of bread, but people were desperate to survive.

Headlines in the *Halifax Herald*, 1925.

Children, in particular, were suffering. Without money or credit at the company store, parents couldn't feed or clothe their children properly. Lack of food led to starving children who caught diseases like tuberculosis more easily. Lack of proper clothing meant children had to wear cement and flour bags Shoes were a luxury that workers couldn't afford for their families. Without enough food and clothing, children couldn't attend school. Worse, they were dying, more than anywhere else in the whole country. Sara Gold, a social worker who went to Cape Breton during this time, wrote a report of the conditions she witnessed in the community:

> *Not one of them have outer clothing but what they wear. There is no change of underwear for anyone, and the children wear none at all; I found them in bed*

trying to keep warm, with thin cotton dresses against their little bare bodies. They had that winter not been to school or outdoors, for they had no boots or stockings. The miner, his wife and the older children have bad teeth and red defective eyes. The children have diseased throats and breathe badly.

"They can't stand the gaff"

Roy the Wolf didn't care that children were sick, starving, and dying. He didn't care that families had no way to provide for themselves. He just wanted to pay even lower wages. News was travelling about the alarming situation in the Cape Breton coalfields. Halifax, Ottawa, and Winnipeg newspapers ran headlines speaking out about the suffering of the desperate communities.

A soldier guarding the colliery during the 1925 strike.

Fight On!

The Red Cross organized relief packages, and donations came in from across the country to help the starving families.

Even though the situation was very serious, neither the provincial government nor the federal government would force Wolvin to talk to the union. Then J. E. McClurg, vice-president of BESCO, made an outrageous statement: "Game of poker-nothing. We hold the cards…let them stay out for two months or six months it matters not, eventually they will have to come to us…they can't stand the gaff." "Standing the gaff" became a famous expression in Cape Breton. McClurg meant that he didn't think the miners and their families were strong enough to survive the extreme poverty and hardships of striking. He figured they would go back to work in a short time. He knew even less about the determination of the Cape Breton miners than he did about working in a mine. The miners and their families were brave and committed and they were certainly willing to "stand the gaff" for as long as it would take to fight for a living wage.

The Battle of Waterford Lake

All through the long, cold months of late winter and early spring, the strike dragged on. The corporation wouldn't meet with the union leaders. By June, nothing had changed. The union decided it was time to take maintenance workers from the power plant. On the morning of June 4, the miners working at the power station walked off the job.

The 1925 Strike

Still the company refused to compromise or consider the starving families. Instead, a week later, they once again sent a special police force to Cape Breton to recapture the power plant at Waterford Lake. The company police came on horseback, carrying guns and batons, and recaptured the plant from the workers occupying it. Once the company had regained control, they restored power to the mines but not to the town of New Waterford.

The Royal Canadian Dragoons, sent to Cape Breton during the 1925 strike, as a show of force against the miners.

Now there was no power, families were starving, and they didn't even have drinking water! The New Waterford Hospital needed water to take care of its patients. The miners' union organized a line to hand pail after pail of water from a local well all the way to the hospital to help relieve the suffering of the sick and dying.

Fight On!

The community couldn't stand it any longer. Miners and their wives and even children gathered and marched out to Waterford Lake to take back the power plant. As they approached, the company police charged the crowd on horseback, attacking them with nightsticks and guns. In the bloody battle that followed, many miners were injured, and one miner, William Davis, was shot dead.

His death made the miners furious. They stormed the power plant and ripped out the main board so it couldn't work. They charged into the company stores, emptying them and then setting them on fire. They even set fire to some of the colliery buildings. They wanted to send a message by damaging the property that the company valued over the lives of the struggling workers and their families.

William Davis's death was a tragedy for his family and for the whole community. Davis had been a hardworking miner

Headline from the *Halifax Herald*, 1925.

since he was a young man. He had lost his older brother to a mine disaster. His death left behind a very poor wife and nine children. William Davis became a symbol of the miners' long, hard fight for justice. The Battle of Waterford Lake, as it came to be called, was an event that would never be forgotten in the coal communities of Cape Breton. June 11 was named "Davis Day"; each year the community would honour William Davis and the miners' struggle. Today it is known as "William Davis Miners' Memorial Day," and it is still observed by Nova Scotian mining communities.

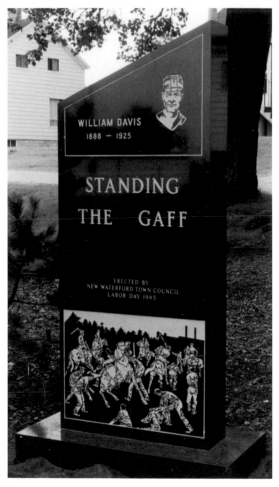

Erected in New Waterford in 1985, this statue is a tribute to William Davis and to the labour struggles of all miners. The scene depicts the Battle of Waterford Lake, where Davis was shot.

Fight On!

CHAPTER 6
The Workers' Legacy

What came out of the 1925 strike?

Even after the Battle of Waterford Lake, the strike did not end. Wolvin wouldn't compromise. In July, the new Conservative provincial government, led by E. N. Rhodes, was sworn into office, and after a few weeks, Rhodes finally worked out a settlement. The miners accepted a 6 to 8 percent wage reduction instead of 10 percent, BESCO had to rehire all striking miners without creating a blacklist, and, very importantly, BESCO had to recognize the union. The company didn't offer much, but it was the first time they'd offered anything since the strike had begun. The miners accepted. After five months, the strike was over. In addition, there would be a royal commission to investigate the coal-mining industry in Nova Scotia and McLachlan would be a key witness.

It was the end of company stores. They were never rebuilt again. It was the beginning of the end of BESCO, which collapsed in 1926. And Roy "the Wolf" Wolvin, who had lost the company a lot of money and caused more suffering to the coal communities of Cape Breton than anyone else, was forced to resign.

During the royal commission, McLachlan was questioned by Roy the Wolf himself. When Wolf implied that McLachlan was spreading Communist propaganda among children, McLachlan replied: "I believe in telling children the truth about the history of the world, that it does not consist in the history of Kings and Lords and Cabinets, but consists in the history of the mass of the workers, a thing that is not taught in the schools. I believe in telling children how to measure value, a thing that is not taught in any school."

J. B. McLachlan and the coal-mining families of Cape Breton built solidarity by resisting the corporation and defending their communities. They were willing to "stand the gaff" in the ongoing labour struggles. They would not be silenced and exploited by corporations. They had won the battle for the union of their choice and would continue to fight for fair wages and safe working conditions.

Bend, Labor, bend; pick up your cross;
Bend, break and bleed to feed the Boss;
Bend, break and bleed? Ah, damn it, NO!
Fight on, fight on; let's go, LET'S GO!
—from "The Case of Jim McLachlan" by Dawn Fraser

And fight on they did!

Fight On!

Timeline

1826: The General Mining Association, a British mining company, is given rights to the Cape Breton coalfields. They remain there until 1858, when their rights are revoked.

1879: The Provincial Workmen's Association, the miners' first union, is formed.

1893: William Melville Whitney forms the Dominion Coal Company. The government of Nova Scotia gives the company a ninety-nine-year lease on the land for mining.

1889: Sydney Mines is incorporated as a town.

1901: Glace Bay is incorporated as a town. Whitney forms the Dominion Iron and Steel Company and builds a steel plant in the Whitney Pier area of Sydney.

1902: James Bryson McLachlan arrives from Scotland, landing in Sydney Mines. He becomes active in fighting for worker rights and will go on to become one of the most important labour leaders in the region.

1906: Dominion is incorporated as a town.

1909: Henry Melville Whitney pulls out of the Dominion Coal Company and it is taken over by financiers in Toronto and Montreal. For the first time the miners vote for the union of their choice. McLachlan becomes secretary-treasurer of the first branch of the United Mine Workers of America, District 26 in Glace Bay.

1909–10: The miners go out on strike in July 1909. The strike drags on for months, continuing through the bitterly cold winter. Families have little food and clothing and many are thrown out of their homes because they cannot pay the rent. After ten months, the strike ends in April.

1913: New Waterford becomes incorporated as a town.

1917: July 25 marks the worst mine explosion in Cape Breton history. Sixty-five men and boys die. In the inquiry following the accident, it is found that the managers neglected safety conditions and ignored miners' concerns.

1919: United Mine Workers of America, UMWA, receives recognition.

1920: Roy Mitchell Wolvin (Roy the Wolf) becomes president of

Fight On!

Dominion Iron and Steel Company. Amalgamating the Nova Scotia Steel and Coal Company, he calls the new corporation the British Empire Steel Corporation, or BESCO.

1921: McLachlan launches the *Maritime Labor Herald*, a labour paper devoted to expressing the working-class perspective.

1922: Wolvin announces a 33 percent wage reduction. The miners strike against the starvation wages.

1923: The steelworkers go out on strike for the first time. The government sends troops to Cape Breton to threaten the population. The miners go on a sympathy strike.

1924: The miners strike against wage slashes.

1925: The 1924 contract expires and Wolvin announces wage reductions again. The miners go on a 100 percent strike against the starvation wages. In what will become known as the Battle of Waterford Lake, company police battle with miners over control of the power plant. Many miners are hurt and William Davis is killed.

1926: BESCO begins to fall apart. Roy Wolvin resigns.

Glossary

afterdamp: The poisonous gases that fill the mine after an explosion caused by firedamp, or flammable gases.

bankhead: The building at the opening to the mine where the coal is unloaded and dumped onto mine screens and readied for railway transportation.

blacklist: A list of people whom an authority, such as government or company owners, consider a threat. It can be used to discriminate against people by blocking them from getting work.

coalfields: A region containing coal deposits.

colliery: The mining plant as a whole, including the underground and above-ground workings of the mining area.

colonial: Relating to a colony, which is a country or territory under full or partial control by another country, often far away, with settlers from that country claiming land.

corporation: The modern version of a business in an industrial society, recognized by government.

down the pit: Underground in the tunnels of the mine.

industrial capitalism: An economy based on the production of a large amount of goods, such as coal, in businesses where large numbers of workers are employed and earn their wages.

industrialization: The transformation of a society because of industrial growth.

investor: People who put money, sometimes called "capital," into a project, expecting to make a profit in return.

living wage: The minimum income necessary for workers to meet their basic needs and have a decent quality of life.

outcrop seam: The exposed seams of coal along the shoreline.

pithead: The area around the entrance to a mine shaft.

rake: The travelling boxes that carry workers into and out of the mines.

referendum: A vote in which people are asked to give their opinion on an important political question.

repressive: Controlling people in a severe way by obstructing their freedom.

Glossary

scab: A worker used by a company to replace a striking union worker.

seam: A layer of coal, also called a vein.

shaft: The vertical opening to the mine that connects the surface to the mine tunnels.

solidarity: A sense of unity and shared interests among people organized around a common cause.

union: An organization of workers formed to protect their interests in regards to safety, wages, and other rights.

Resources

Children's Books

Barkhouse, Joyce. *Pit Pony*. Toronto: Gage, 1990.

MacDonald, Hugh R. *Trapper Boy*. Sydney, NS: Cape Breton University Press, 2012.

MacDonald, Hugh R. *Us and Them*. Sydney: Cape Breton University Press, 2013.

General Books

Frank, David. *J. B. McLachlan: A Biography: The story of a legendary labour leader and the Cape Breton coal miners*. Toronto: Lorimer, 1999.

Fraser, Dawn. *Echoes from Labor's Wars Expanded Edition*. Wreck Cove, NS: Breton Books, 1992.

MacIsaac, Teresa. *A Better Life: A Portrait of Highland Women in Nova Scotia*. Sydney: Cape Breton University Press, 2006.

MacKenzie, Rennie. *Blast! Cape Breton Coal Mining Disasters*. Wreck Cove: Breton Books, 2007.

MacKenzie, Rennie. *That Bloody Cape Breton Coal: Stories of Mining Disasters in Everyday Life*. Wreck Cove: Breton Books, 2004.

McIntosh, Robert. *Boys in the Pits*. Montreal and Kingston: McGill-Queen's University Press, 2000.

McNeil, Ian. *Pit Talk: The Legacy of Cape Breton's Coal Miners*. ICON Communications & Research, 2010.

Mellor, John. *The Company Store: J.B. McLachlan and the Cape Breton Coal Miners 1900-1925.* Wreck Cove: Breton Books, 1983 (revised edition, 2012).

Morgan, Robert J. *Rise Again! The Story of Cape Breton: Book 1.* Wreck Cove: Breton Books, 2008.

Morgan, Robert J. *Rise Again! The Story of Cape Breton: Book 2.* Wreck Cove: Breton Books, 2009.

Magazine Articles

The interviews in Ron Caplan's *Cape Breton's Magazine* are a rich source of oral history. Many were consulted for this book. The *Cape Breton's Magazine* archives can be found at www.capebretonsmagazine.com. Look for:

"The Mine Explosion in New Waterford, 1917," issue 21

"1923 Steelworkers' Strike and the Miners Sympathy Strike," issue 22

"With Margaret MacDonald of Glace Bay," issue 25

"Serving on the Mine Rescue Team," issue 31

"European Impact on the Micmac Culture," issue 31

"Horses in the Coal Mines," issue 32

"Early History of the Coal Trade," issues 35 and 36 (excerpt from *The Coal Fields and Coal Trade of the Island of Cape Breton*)

"From Company Town to Labour Town" issue 37

"A Social Worker Visits Cape Breton, 1925," issue 38 (originally appeared in *Social Welfare*, August–September, 1925)

"The Steel Boom Comes to Sydney, 1899," issue 39

"Working on the Sydney Coal Pier," issue 44

"Dawn Fraser, Writer: Selections," issue 45

Fight On!

"Edith Pelley, William Davis's Daughter," issue 60

"A Visit with Winston Ruck, Steelworker" issue 60

"J. B. McLachlan: 'Floors That Have Talked to Me'" issue 74

Websites

The Beaton Institute Archives: www.cbu.ca/campus/beaton-institute

Nova Scotia Archives: www.archives.novascotia.ca

Other resources

Duckworth, Martin. 1978. *12,000 Men: Labour's War in the Cape Breton Coalfields.* DVD. National Film Board of Canada.

Men of the Deeps

Many songs have been written about mining history and miners' lives. In Cape Breton there is a choir of retired miners, the only one of its kind in North America, called the Men of the Deeps. The choir has been keeping these songs alive for over fifty years. Listen to them and you will hear miners sing stories of their very own history. Visit them at: www.menofthedeeps.com.

Protest Song and Verse in Cape Breton Island

The Protest Song Project at the Centre for Cape Breton Studies at Cape Breton University is designed to preserve and promote the protest songs and verse that represent the region's rich industrial heritage. Local musicians have recorded a sampling of some of the amazing songs written about the industrial history of Cape Breton. Some of these songs are based on poems by Dawn Fraser, published first in J. B. McLachlan's labour paper, the *Maritime Labor Herald*. Visit: www.protestsongs.ca.

The Miners Museum

Here, you can visit a real coal mine. When I was a kid I went to the Miners Museum in Glace Bay many times. It is where I really came to understand the labour history of mining. If you want to know what it felt like to go down the pit, visit the museum and take a tour underground with a retired miner. If you get a chance to go, you'll never forget it. Visit: www.minersmuseum.com.

'There's Herring in the Bay'

We noticed a man walking up Main Street today with a nice looking string or gad of fresh herring. As he was coming from the general direction of the water front we assume that these popular delicacies were caught somewhere within our 3-mile limit. Natural resources as it were. Considering the short time that is anticipated at the Mines this summer the sight of the herring was reassuring and it is a comfort to contemplate if the worst comes to the worst.——Well we can put a herring in the pot. Fellow who lives down Antigonish way tells me he lived on herring all last winter. Hot damn a man is never stuck!

Maritime Labor Herald, 1924.

Fight On!

Image Credits

Page 5: Coal Miners, Dominion No. 1 Colliery, Dominion, ca. 1900. 86-334-16532. Beaton Institute, Cape Breton University.

Page 6: Dominion Colliery No. 2, Glace Bay, 1912. 77-1250-1384. Beaton Institute, Cape Breton University.

Page 7 (top): Blast Furnace Boiler Room, Dominion Iron & Steel Company, Sydney, 1900. 77-53-187. Beaton Institute, Cape Breton University.
Page 7 (bottom): Dominion Iron and Steel Company, ca. 1905. 79-970-3950a. Beaton Institute, Cape Breton University.

Page 10: Dominion No. 6 Bankhead, ca. 1920. 78-142-1892. Beaton Institute, Cape Breton University.

Page 13: Horse Haulage #20 Colliery, Glace Bay, 1952. Photograph by Shedden Studio. 77-698-832. Beaton Institute, Cape Breton University.

Page 14: Miners (boys) at Caledonia, ca. 1903. 80-5-4185. Beaton Institute, Cape Breton University.

Page 18: Coal Company House, n.d. -459-7159. Beaton Institute, Cape Breton University.

Page 20: Dominion Coal Company Store, Caledonia, ca. 1912. 80-13-4193. Beaton Institute, Cape Breton University.

Page 21: Paysheet for Joseph P. MacLean, Reserve Colliery, July 16, 1909. MG 14.26 A. viii (a). Beaton Institute, Cape Breton University.

Page 23: James Bryson (J.B.) McLachlan, 1933. Photograph by Shedden Studio. 76-84a. Beaton Institute, Cape Breton University.

Page 27: Coal Mine, Dominion, 1907. 78-105-1855. Beaton Institute, Cape Breton University.

Page 28: Army officers stationed at Dominion No 3., Glace Bay during 1909 coal strike, July 12, 1909. 78-735-2485. Beaton Institute, Cape Breton University.

Page 30: Donkin Miners, ca. 1925. 86-68-16165. Beaton Institute, Cape Breton University.

Page 33: Dräeger Crew, No. 2 and No. 9 Colliery, Glace Bay, 1909. Photographer unknown. 76-102. Beaton Institute, Cape Breton University.

Page 37: Plummer Avenue, New Waterford, ca. 1915. 80-4-4184. Beaton Institute, Cape Breton University.

Page 38 (top): Men and Shovels at Dominion #6, ca. 1920. 78-149-1899. Beaton Institute, Cape Breton University.

Page 38 (bottom): British Empire Steel Corporation, No. 2 Colliery, Glace Bay, ca. 1921. Photographer unknown. Reference number: 80-2-4182. Beaton Institute, Cape Breton University.

Page 45: Sydney Steel Plant Strike, ca. 1923. 89-510-18705. Beaton Institute, Cape Breton University.

Page 54: Strikers, 1925. Photograph by Abbass Studios Ltd. 563.1. Beaton Institute, Cape Breton University.

Page 56: Royal Canadian Dragoons at Sydney Steel Plant, ca. 1925. 87-964-17494. Beaton Institute, Cape Breton University.

Acknowledgements

My sincere thank you to the whole team at Nimbus, most especially to Whitney Moran for her interest and unflagging support for this book, to Penelope Jackson for her excellent edit, and to Emily MacKinnon for pulling it all together.

I am deeply indebted to the work of a few key people who have documented the mining history in Cape Breton. I first read John Mellor's passionate history, *The Company Store*, in my twenties and it left an enduring impression. I later read David Frank's fascinating biography of J. B. McLachlan and his many other writings about Cape Breton labour struggles in the early twentieth century. His work is indispensible. To them and to the several other significant Cape Breton historians I have read and learned from: I am grateful.

Ronald Caplan's *Cape Breton's Magazine* and books from his press, Breton Books, have been invaluable resources. The first-hand accounts from the people who actually lived this experience are the closest thing to being there.

A very special thank you to Anna MacNeil and Jane Arnold of the Beaton Institute for their very helpful research assistance. Thank you also to Lachlan MacKinnon at Cape Breton University for his careful reading and commentary.

I would also like to acknowledge my grandmother, Rose Schwartz, who arrived in New Waterford in 1913, the year it was incorporated as a town. She lived through this history and was deeply sympa-

Maritime Labor Herald, 1924.

thetic to the miners. The family's small store, which eventually became a cornerstone business in New Waterford, advertised in the *Maritime Labor Herald*—a true sign of supporting the cause of workers' rights. And to my father, Irving Schwartz, who throughout his life spoke about his great respect for the miners and their families. He passed on that legacy and it has inspired the writing of this book.

Finally, my deepest thank you to Marco Fonseca for the many stimulating conversations, wise insights, and unwavering encouragement for this project. It has made all the difference.

Fight On!